Watch it Grow

An Oak Tree's Life

Nancy Dickmann

www.raintreepublishers.co.uk
Visit our website to find out more information about Raintree books.

To order:
Phone 0845 6044371
Fax +44 (0) 1865 312263
Email myorders@raintreepublishers.co.uk

Customers from outside the UK please telephone +44 1865 312262

Raintree is an imprint of Capstone Global Library Limited, a company incorporated in England and Wales having its registered office at 7 Pilgrim Street, London, EC4V 6LB – Registered company number: 6695582

Edited by Nancy Dickmann, Rebecca Rissman, and Catherine Veitch
Designed by Joanna Hinton-Malivoire
Picture research by Mica Brancic
Production by Victoria Fitzgerald
Originated by Capstone Globa Library Ltd
Printed and bound in China by South China Printing Company Ltd

ISBN 978 0 431 19540 7
14 13 12 11 10
10 9 8 7 6 5 4 3 2 1

British Library Cataloguing in Publication Data
Dickmann, Nancy.
Oak tree. -- (Watch it grow)
583.4'6-dc22

Acknowledgements
We would would like to thank the following for permission to reproduce photographs: iStockphoto pp. **5** (© Kjell Brynildsen), **6** (© Andrew Cribb), **7** (© Georges Mauger), **8** (© Dirk Freder), **13** (eurobanks), **14** (© Anthony Brown), **15** (© Hans F. Meier), **18** (© Achim Prill), **22 left** (© Achim Prill), **23 middle bottom** (© Dirk Freder); Photolibrary pp. **4** (Flirt Collection/ © Ariel Skelley), **9** (imagebroker.net/© Christian Hütter), **10** (Garden Picture Library/Frederic Didillon), **11** (Garden Picture Library/© James Guilliam), **12** (age fotostock/© Javier Larrea), **16** (© Radius Images), **22 bottom** (© Radius Images), **22 right** (Garden Picture Library/© James Guilliam), **22 top** (imagebroker.net/© Christian Hütter) **23 top** (© Radius Images), **23 middle top** (Garden Picture Library/Frederic Didillon), **23 bottom** (Garden Picture Library/© James Guilliam); Shutterstock pp. **17** (© istera), **19** (© Antonio S.), **20** (© IDAL), **21** (© Alexander Chelmodeev).

Front cover photograph (main) of an oak tree in a meadow reproduced with permission of Shutterstock (© Igor Normann). Front cover photograph (inset) of two acorns in the sun reproduced with permission of iStockphoto (© Achim Prill). Back cover photograph of an acorn reproduced with permission of Photolibrary (imagebroker.net/© Christian Hütter).

The publisher would like to thank Nancy Harris for her assistance in the preparation of this book.

Every effort has been made to contact copyright holders of material reproduced in this book. Any omissions will be rectified in subsequent printings if notice is given to the publisher.

Contents

Life cycles

All living things have a life cycle.

An oak tree has a life cycle.

An oak tree starts as a tiny acorn.

The acorn grows into a tall tree.
Later the tree will die.

Seeds and shoots

An acorn has a seed inside it.

The seed grows in the ground.

Roots grow down from the seed into the ground.

A shoot and leaves grow from the seed.

Becoming a tree

The young tree needs water and sunlight to grow.

The young tree grows bigger.

The tree grows new leaves in the spring.

The leaves change colour and die in the autumn.

Making acorns

Catkins grow on the oak tree in the spring.

Acorns grow from the catkins.

A seed grows inside each acorn.

Squirrels eat some acorns.

Some acorns fall to the ground.

The life cycle starts again.

Life cycle of an oak tree

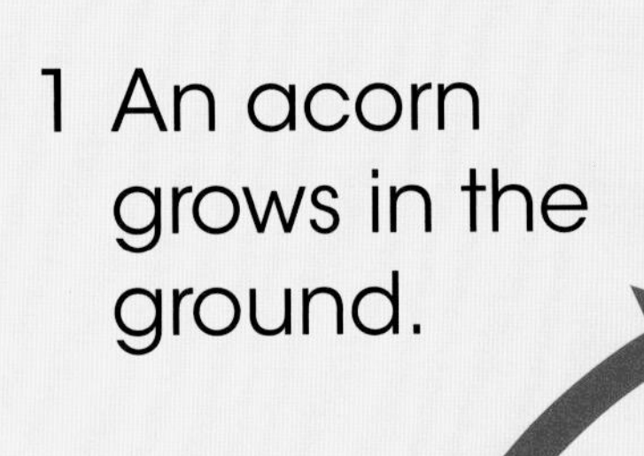

1 An acorn grows in the ground.

2 The young tree grows leaves and branches.

3 Catkins grow on the tree.

4 Acorns grow from the catkins.

Picture glossary

catkin long, flowery part that grows on an oak tree in spring

root part of a plant that grows underground. Roots take up water for the plant to use.

seed tiny thing that grows into a new plant. Plants make seeds.

shoot small green stem that grows from a seed

Index

Notes to parents and teachers

Before reading

Show the children some acorns and see if they know what they are. Do they know a place where they could find acorns? Ask them if they know what acorns grow into.

After reading

- Show the children an oak leaf and explain that different trees have different shaped leaves. Then show them leaves (or pictures of leaves) from a horse chestnut tree, a beech tree, a sycamore tree, and a field maple tree. Do they know which trees these leaves are from? When you have identified the leaves together, show them a conker, a beech nut, and sycamore and maple seeds, and ask them to match them with the leaves. Ask them why they think the conker and beech nut cases are prickly. Why do they think the sycamore and maple seeds are like helicopters?
- Tell the children that acorns are a good energy food for squirrels and other animals. Go on a nature walk to a local park or woodland and look for squirrels. Can the children see them finding and eating acorns? What else do they eat? Can the children see any young trees growing from fallen acorns?